ISBN 978-1-5284-2275-8
PIBN 10901505

1 MONTH OF
FREE
READING

at
www.ForgottenBooks.com

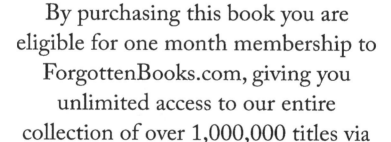

By purchasing this book you are eligible for one month membership to ForgottenBooks.com, giving you unlimited access to our entire collection of over 1,000,000 titles via our web site and mobile apps.

To claim your free month visit:
www.forgottenbooks.com/free901505

English
Français
Deutsche
Italiano
Español
Português

www.forgottenbooks.com

Mythology Photography **Fiction**
Fishing Christianity **Art** Cooking
Essays Buddhism Freemasonry
Medicine **Biology** Music **Ancient
Egypt** Evolution Carpentry Physics
Dance Geology **Mathematics** Fitness
Shakespeare **Folklore** Yoga Marketing
Confidence Immortality Biographies
Poetry **Psychology** Witchcraft
Electronics Chemistry History **Law**
Accounting **Philosophy** Anthropology
Alchemy Drama Quantum Mechanics
Atheism Sexual Health **Ancient History**
Entrepreneurship Languages Sport
Paleontology Needlework Islam
Metaphysics Investment Archaeology
Parenting Statistics Criminology
Motivational

Historic, archived document

Do not assume content reflects current
scientific knowledge, policies, or practices.

Bridgeport, Marion County, Indiana, Since 1875

141 Years in the Same Family

PRICE LIST
Spring 1953

This Price List contains a complete list of our 1953 Spring
Stock. Please make up your order from this price list. For
detailed description consult our illustrated color catalogue.

C. M. HOBBS & SONS, Inc.

Phones: Indianapolis BElmont 1812; Plainfield 2644

QUALITY STOCK AT REASONABLE PRICES

WITHOUT TREES AND SHRUBS IT IS ONLY A HOUSE—
WITH THEM A HOME

✦✦✦✦✦✦✦

DRIVE OUT AND VISIT OUR NURSERIES

Concrete Road from Indianapolis to Our Office

A straight drive of only nine miles from Meridian Street directly West on Washington Street (Old National Road or Terre Haute Road) U.S. No. 40

Hourly Bus Service from Indianapolis

We Do Not Sell Through Agents

✦✦✦✦✦✦✦

MEMBERS OF

AMERICAN ASSOCIATION OF NURSERYMEN
INDIANA ASSOCIATION OF NURSERYMEN
INDIANAPOLIS LANDSCAPE ASSOCIATION

SUBSTITUTION

We have found many of our customers desire us to fill their orders complete by using our good judgement in selecting varieties for them in case we were short of varieties ordered. Many times we can better the selection, but if you do not wish us to use our judgment in selecting varieties to take the place of those that may be exhausted, kindly mark on the face of your order, "No Substitution", and we will gladly refund balance of your remittance.

LOCATION

Six miles from the west corporate line of Indianapolis, on Washington Street, on the Old National Road (U.S. 40), Pennsylvania Railroad. Hourly Bus Service from Indianapolis.

PHONES

Indianapolis: BElmont 1812; Plainfield 2644

VISITORS

You are always welcome and we will be pleased to meet you and show you through our plant, comprising more than 400 acres.

SHIPPING FACILITIES

Pennsylvania Railroad making connection with all lines out of Indianapolis. Ample facilities for shipment by motor freight.

SHIPPING INSTRUCTIONS

ORDERS—All orders are accepted subject to the following terms and conditions. Write plainly and give explicit directions as to address and mode of shipment.

FORWARDING—Shipments will be forwarded exactly as directed; but, where without instructions, we will use our best judgement and forward by shortest and safest route. We recommend that all herbaceous and strawberry plants be shipped by express.

CLAIMS—For damage while in transit or otherwise must be made within five days after the arrival of the consignment.

SHIPPING SEASON—Opens about March 1st in the spring and September 1st in the fall.

INSPECTION AND FUMIGATION—Our stock is regularly inspected and certificate will be sent with each shipment.

PACKING—All goods are carefully packed, thus avoiding risk if delayed in transit. We do not charge for packing.

TERMS

CASH WITH ORDER—Except to persons who satisfy us as to their financial responsibility. Accounts are due when bills are rendered, and prompt payments are expected.

PRICES given in this catalog are for the goods F.O.B., Bridgeport, Indiana. STOCK selected by our customers at the nurseries will be charged for according to the value of the trees or plants chosen.

EVERGREENS

All evergreens balled and burlapped, transplanted, nursery grown

ARBOR VITAE

AMERICAN DARK GREEN (Upright)

Each

18 to 24 inch	$ 3.00
2 to 2½ feet	3.50
2½ to 3 feet	4.50

GLOBE

12 to 15 inch	3.00
15 to 18 inch	3.25

ORIENTALIS

18 to 24 inch	2.75
2 to 2½ feet	3.00
2½ to 3 feet	3.50
3 to 3½ feet	4.00
3½ to 4 feet	5.00

ORIENTALIS COMPACTA

18 to 24 inch	3.00
2 to 2½ feet	3.50
3 to 3½ feet	5.00

PYRAMIDALIS (Upright)

18 to 24 inch	3.00
2 to 2½ feet	3.50
2½ to 3 feet	4.50
3 to 3½ feet	5.00
3½ to 4 feet	6.00
4 to 4½ feet	7.00
4½ to 5 feet	8.00
5 to 6 feet	9.00

SIBERIAN

15 to 18 inch	2.50
18 to 24 inch	3.00

BIOTA

AUREA NANA (Yellow Foliage)

12 to 15 inch	2.75

FIR

BALSAM

18 to 24 inch	3.00
2 to 2½ feet	3.75
2½ to 3 feet	4.50

DOUGLASS

2 to 2½ feet	4.50
2½ to 3 feet	5.00
3 to 3½ feet	6.00

Part of a block of Juniper Glauca (left) and Cannarti (right) showing well-shaped evergreens as the result of expert shearing.

JUNIPER

Each

BURKI (Upright)

	Each
2 to 2½ feet	4.50
2½ to 3 feet	5.25
3 to 3½ feet	6.25

CANNARTI (Pyramidal)

	Each
3½ to 4 feet	7.50
4 to 4½ feet	8.50
4½ to 5 feet	10.00
5 to 6 feet	12.00

COLUMNARIS (Pyramidal)

	Each
2 to 2½ feet	5.00
2½ to 3 feet	6.00
3 to 3½ feet	6.50

DEPRESSA PLUMOSA (Spreading)

	Each
15 to 18 inch	4.00
18 to 24 inch	4.50
2 to 2½ feet	5.50

GLAUCA (Blue Foliage, Upright)

	Each
3 to 3½ feet	6.50
3½ to 4 feet	7.50
4 to 4½ feet	8.50
4½ to 5 feet	10.00
5 to 6 feet	12.00

A block of Upright Juniper grafts. Note the uniform well-sheared varieties of of Keteleri, Columnaris and Mascula.

FASTIGIATA

18 to 24 inch	2.25
2 to 2½ feet	3.00
2½ to 3 feet	3.25

IRISH (Pyramidal)

18 to 24 inch	2.25
2 to 2½ feet	2.75
2½ to 3 feet	3.25
3 to 3½ feet	3.75

KETELERI

2 to 2½ feet	4.00
2½ to 3 feet	5.00
3 to 3½ feet	6.00
3½ to 4 feet	7.00
4 to 4½ feet	8.00

MASCULA

2 to 2½ feet	5.00
2½ to 3 feet	6.00
3 to 3½ feet	7.00

MEYERI

12 to 15 inch	3.00

PFITZERIANA (Spreading)

15 to 18 inch	4.00
18 to 24 inch	5.00

A block of Pfitzer Juniper which has been partly dug out showing the compact growth throughout the evergreen assuring a uniform grade.

JUNIPER (Continued)

Each

PFITZER COMPACTA

	Each
12 to 15 inch	3.50
15 to 18 inch	4.00

PFITZER HETZI

15 to 18 inch	3.75
18 to 24 inch	4.75
2 to 2½ feet	5.50
2½ to 3 feet	6.00

PYRAMIDIFORMA (Dundee, Pyramidal)

2 to 2½ feet	4.50
2½ to 3 feet	5.50

SCHOTTI

3 to 3½ feet	6.50
3½ to 4 feet	7.50
4 to 4½ feet	8.50

STRICTA

12 to 15 inch	2.75
15 to 18 inch	3.50
18 to 24 inch	4.50
2 to 2½ feet	5.00

VON EHRON — Each

15 to 18 inch	3.75
18 to 24 inch	4.75
2 to 2½ feet	5.75
2½ to 3 feet	6.75

PINE (Grow large, need room)

AUSTRIAN

2 to 3 feet	6.00

SCOTCH

2 to 3 feet	6.00
3 to 4 feet	7.50
4 to 5 feet	14.00

SPRUCE

BLACK HILL

18 to 24 inch	3.00
2 to 2½ feet	4.00

KOSTER BLUE SPRUCE

2½ to 3 feet	20.00
3 to 3½ feet	25.00
3½ to 4 feet	30.00
4 to 4½ feet	35.00

NORWAY

18 to 24 inch	2.75
2 to 2½ feet	3.75
2½ to 3 feet	4.75
3 to 3½ feet	5.75

TAXUS (Good in shade or sun)

ANDERSONI

15 to 18 inch	7.00
18 to 24 inch	9.00

BROWNI

15 to 18 inch	7.00

CAPITATA (Pyramidal)

18 to 24 inch	7.50
2 to 2½ feet	9.50
2½ to 3 feet	13.00
3 to 3½ feet	18.00
3½ to 4 feet	20.00
4 to 4½ feet	30.00
4½ to 5 feet	35.00

CUSPIDATA (Spreading)

15 to 18 inch	7.00
18 to 24 inch	9.00

HATFIELD

15 to 18 inch	5.75
18 to 24 inch	6.75

HICKSI (Upright)

15 to 18 inch	6.00
18 to 24 inch	7.50

HONNEWELLIANA

15 to 18 inch	7.00

INTERMEDIA (Spreading)

15 to 18 inch	7.00

TAXUS (Continued)

Each

VERMULEUN

15 to 18 inch	5.75
18 to 24 inch	6.75
2 to 2½ feet	8.00

HEMLOCK

3 to 3½ feet	8.50
3½ to 4 feet	10.00
4 to 4½ feet	12.00

BROADLEAF EVERGREENS

BARBERRY

Each

JULIANAE

12 to 15 inch (B & B)	2.50
15 to 18 inch (B & B)	3.00
18 to 24 inch (B & B)	3.50

MENTORENSIS

12 to 15 inch	.85
15 to 18 inch	1.00
18 to 24 inch	1.20
2 to 3 feet	1.50

EUONYMUS

PATENS (Upright Dwarf)

18 to 24 inch (B & B)	4.00

RADICANS ERECTUS

12 to 15 inch (B & B)	2.50

VEGETUS (Spreading)

12 to 15 inch (B & B)	2.50

ILEX

CRENATA

18 to 24 inch (B & B)	6.50

CRENATA CONVEXA

15 to 18 inch (B & B)	5.50
18 to 24 inch (B & B)	6.50

GLABRA

12 to 15 inch (B & B)	3.00
15 to 18 inch (B & B)	3.50

OPACA (American Holly)

3 to 4 feet (B & B)	9.00
4 to 5 feet (B & B)	11.50

ROTUNDIFOLIA

15 to 18 inch (B & B)	5.50
18 to 24 inch (B & B)	6.50

MAHONIA AQUIFOLIA

12 to 15 inch (B & B)	3.00
15 to 18 inch (B & B)	3.75

VIBURNUM

BURKWOODI

18 to 24 inch (B & B)	3.75
2 to 3 feet (Cloverset Pots)	4.25

DECIDUOUS TREES

Feet refers to height of tree; inch refers to diameter of tree; B & B trees are dug with a ball of earth and burlapped. (All trees listed over 8/10 feet have been root pruned within last two and three years.)

ASH

AMERICAN WHITE
	Each
5 to 6 feet	2.00
6 to 8 feet	2.25
8 to 10 feet	3.00

EUROPEAN MOUNTAIN (Orange Berries in Fall)
4 to 5 feet	2.50
5 to 6 feet	3.00
6 to 8 feet	3.50
8 to 10 feet	4.00
1¼ to 1½ inch	5.50
1½ to 2 inch	7.00

BIRCH

CUT LEAF WEEPING
5 to 6 feet (B &B)	4.50
6 to 8 feet (B & B)	6.00
8 to 10 feet (B & B)	7.50
10 to 12 feet (B & B)	9.00
1½ to 2 inch (B & B)	11.00

CHERRY—Flowering Kwanzan
3 to 4 feet	3.00
4 to 5 feet	4.00

CHINESE CHESTNUT
3 to 4 feet	3.50
4 to 5 feet	4.00

CORNUS FLORIDA (Dogwood)

WHITE FLOWERING
18 to 24 inch (B & B)	3.50
2 to 3 feet (B & B)	4.00
3 to 4 feet (B & B)	5.00
4 to 5 feet (B & B)	7.00
5 to 6 feet (B & B)	9.00

RED FLOWERING
18 to 24 inch (B & B)	4.50
2 to 3 feet (B & B)	5.00
3 to 4 feet (B & B)	7.00

CRAB—Flowering

(Atrosanguinea, Dolga, Eleyi, Hopa, Sargenti, Scheideckeri, Spectabilis, Zumi Calicarpi)
In Variety, 3 to 4 feet (B & B $ .80 extra)	1.50
In Variety, 4 to 5 feet (B & B $1.00 extra)	1.75
In Variety, 5 to 6 feet (B & B $1.50 extra)	2.25
In Variety, 6 to 7 feet (B & B $2.50 extra)	3.00

BECHTELS DBL. FLG.
2 to 3 feet (B & B .70 extra)	1.50
3 to 4 feet (B & B .80 extra)	2.00
4 to 5 feet (B & B 1.00 extra)	2.75
5 to 6 feet (B & B 1.50 extra)	3.50

Several rows of Pink Dogwood trees.

FLOWERING PEACH (Red)

	Each
2 to 3 feet	1.25
3 to 4 feet	1.75
4 to 5 feet	2.00
5 to 6 feet	2.50

ELM (CHINESE)

	Each	5 to 49 Each
4 to 5 feet	1.75	1.50
5 to 6 feet	2.00	1.75
6 to 8 feet	2.75	2.50
8 to 10 feet	3.25	3.00
1¼ to 1½ inch	4.50	4.00
1½ to 2 inch	5.50	5.00
2 to 2½ inch	7.50	
2½ to 3 inch	9.50	
3 to 3½ inch	12.00	
3½ to 4 inch	14.00	

GINKGO (Maidenhair Tree)

	Each
4 to 5 feet	2.00
5 to 6 feet	2.75
6 to 8 feet	3.75
8 to 10 feet	5.00
3 to 3½ inch	15.00
3½ to 4 inch	20.00
4 to 4½ inch	25.00

HACKBERRY

5 to 6 feet	2.25
6 to 8 feet	2.50
8 to 10 feet	3.00
1¼ to 1½ inch	4.50
1½ to 2 inch	5.50
2 to 2½ inch	7.50

HONEYLOCUST

THORNLESS

5 to 6 feet	2.50
6 to 8 feet	2.75
8 to 10 feet	3.75
1¼ to 1½ inch	4.50

MORAINE (Thornless, No Seed Pods)

5 to 6 feet	5.00
6 to 8 feet	7.00
8 to 10 feet	8.50

LINDEN (American)

5 to 6 feet	2.25
6 to 8 feet	2.50
8 to 10 feet	3.50

MAGNOLIA

NIGRA

2 to 3 feet (B & B)	6.50
3 to 4 feet (B & B)	9.00
4 to 5 feet (B & B)	10.50

SOULANGEANA (Pink)

2 to 3 feet (B & B)	6.50
3 to 4 feet (B & B)	9.00
4 to 5 feet (B & B)	10.50
5 to 6 feet (B & B)	12.50

MAPLE

BOX ELDER

6 to 8 feet	2.00
1¼ to 1½ inch	4.00
1½ to 2 inch	5.00

CRIMSON KING (Patented)

5 to 6 feet	5.00

GINNALA

3 to 4 feet	1.50
4 to 5 feet	2.00

JAPANESE RED LEAF (Dwarf Ornamental)

15 to 18 inch (B & B)	5.00
18 to 24 inch (B & B)	6.00

Fine specimen Sugar Maple trees

MAPLE (Continued)

Each

NORWAY

6 to 8 feet	4.00
8 to 10 feet	5.00
1¼ to 1½ inch	6.00
1½ to 1¾ inch	7.00
1½ to 2 inch	8.50
2 to 2½ inch	10.00
2½ to 3 inch	13.00
3 to 3½ inch	18.00
3½ to 4 inch	22.00
4 to 4½ inch	26.00
4½ to 5 inch	32.00
5 to 6 inch	40.00

RUBRUM (Red Fall Foliage)

5 to 6 feet	3.50
6 to 8 feet	5.00
8 to 10 feet	6.00
1¼ to 1½ inch	7.50

SCHWEDLERI (Red Spring Foliage)

5 to 6 feet	3.50
6 to 8 feet	5.00

SOFT OR SILVER

	Each
6 to 8 feet	2.25
8 to 10 feet	3.00
1¼ to 1½ inch	3.75

SUGAR

5 to 6 feet	3.50
6 to 8 feet	4.50
8 to 10 feet	5.00
1¼ to 1½ inch	6.00
3½ to 4 inch (B & B $20.00 extra)	25.00
4 to 4½ inch (B & B $25.00 extra)	30.00
4½ to 5 inch (B & B $30.00 extra)	37.50
5 to 6 inch (B & B $35.00 extra)	42.50
6 to 7 inch (B & B $45.00 extra)	50.00

MIMOSA

5 to 6 feet	2.50

OAK

BURR (Macrocarpa)

2½ to 3 inch (B & B $10.00 extra)	15.00
3 to 3½ inch (B & B $15.00 extra)	18.00
3½ to 4 inch (B & B $20.00 extra)	25.00
4 to 4½ inch (B & B $25.00 extra)	30.00

ENGLISH

2½ to 3 inch (B & B $10.00 extra)	15.00
3 to 3½ inch (B& B $15.00 extra)	18.00
3½ to 4 inch (B & B $20.00 extra)	25.00

PIN (Palustris)

5 to 6 feet	4.00
6 to 8 feet	5.00
3½ to 4 inch (B & B $20.00 extra)	25.00
4 to 4½ inch (B & B $25.00 extra)	30.00
4½ to 5 inch (B & B $30.00 extra)	35.00
5 to 6 inch (B & B $35.00 extra)	42.50
6 to 7 inch (B & B $45.00 extra)	50.00

RED (Rubrum)

5 to 6 feet	4.00
6 to 8 feet	5.00
8 to 10 feet	6.50
1¼ to 1½ inch	7.50
3 to 3½ inch (B & B $15.00 extra)	18.00
3½ to 4 inch (B & B $20.00 extra)	25.00
4 to 4½ inch (B & B $25.00 extra)	30.00

SCARLET (Coccinea)

6 to 8 feet	5.00
8 to 10 feet	6.50
1¼ to 1½ inch	7.50
1½ to 2 inch	9.00
2 to 2½ inch	12.00

WHITE (Alba)

3 to 3½ inch (B & B $15.00 extra)	18.00
3½ to 4 inch (B & B $20.00 extra)	25.00
4 to 4½ inch (B & B $25.00 extra)	30.00

POPLAR (Lombardy)

	Each	5 to 49 Each
4 to 5 feet	.60	.50
5 to 6 feet	.75	.60
6 to 8 feet	1.00	.75
8 to 10 feet	1.50	1.00

PRUNUS (Flowering Plum)

Each

⅃ CISTENA
4 to 5 feet 2.00

⅃ NEWPORT
2 to 3 feet 1.50
3 to 4 feet 1.75
4 to 5 feet 2.00
5 to 6 feet 2.50
6 to 7 feet 3.00

RED BUD

2 to 3 feet (B & B $.90 extra) 1.75
3 to 4 feet (B & B $1.25 extra) 2.50
4 to 5 feet B & B $1.50 extra) 3.50
5 to 6 feet (B & B $1.95 extra) 5.00
6 to 7 feet (B & B $2.75 extra) 6.50

RUSSIAN OLIVE

5 to 6 feet 2.25
6 to 8 feet 3.00
8 to 10 feet 4.00

SYCAMORE (Common)

5 to 6 feet 2.50
6 to 8 feet 3.00
8 to 10 feet 3.50

SWEET GUM (Liquidamber)

5 to 6 feet (B & B) 6.50
6 to 8 feet (B & B) 8.00
8 to 10 feet (B & B) 10.00
1¼ to 1½ inch (B & B) 12.50
1½ to 2 inch (B & B) 15.00
2 to 2½ inch (B & B) 20.00
2½ to 3 inch (B & B) 25.00

THORN (CRATAEGUS)

COCCINEA (Thicket Hawthorne)
5 to 6 feet (B & B) 10.50
6 to 8 feet (B & B) 12.50
8 to 10 feet (B &B) 15.00

CORDATA (Washington Hawthorne)
2 to 3 feet (B & B) 5.00
10 to 12 feet (B & B) 18.00

CRUSGALLI (Cockspur Thorn)
3 to 4 feet (B & B) 7.00
4 to 5 feet (B & B) 9.00
5 to 6 feet (B & B) 10.50
6 to 8 feet (B & B) 12.50
8 to 10 feet (B & B) 15.00

PAULS SCARLET
5 to 6 feet 4.00

TULIP TREE

5 to 6 feet (B & B $1.95 extra) 3.50
6 to 8 feet (B & B $2.75 extra) 4.50

WILLOW

	Each	5 to 49 Each
THURLOW (Weeping)		
5 to 6 feet	1.50	1.25
6 to 8 feet	2.00	1.75
8 to 10 feet	2.50	2.00
1¼ to 1½ inch	3.50	3.00

	Each
PUSSY	
4 to 5 feet	1.75
WISCONSIN	
3 to 4 feet	1.00
4 to 5 feet	1.25
5 to 6 feet	1.50
6 to 8 feet	2.00
8 to 10 feet	2.50

TREE WISTERIA

3 to 4 feet (B & B)	7.50

A section of our lath house where small plants are grown under partial shade until large enough to be moved to the fields.

ORNAMENTAL SHRUBS

Most of our shrubs are three and four years old; much more stocky and better than one and two year old plants usually offered.

ALMONDS, PINK

	Each
12 to 18 inch	.85
18 to 24 inch	1.00
2 to 3 feet	1.25

ALPINE CURRANT

12 to 15 inch	.85

ALTHEA (Red, White, Pink, Blue) (Hisbiscus)

2 to 3 feet	.85
3 to 4 feet	1.25
4 to 5 feet	1.50

ARALIA PENTAPHYLLA

2 to 3 feet	.75
3 to 4 feet	.90

ARONIA

ARBUTIFOLIA

2 to 3 feet	1.25

MELANOCARPA

18 to 24 inch	1.00

BARBERRY MENTORENSIS (See Broadleaf Evergreens)

BARBERRY

RED LEAF

	Each	5 to 49 Each
15 to 18 inch	.75	.70
18 to 24 inch	.90	.85

THUNBERGI

	Each	5 to 49 Each
10 to 12 inch	.40	.35
12 to 15 inch	.50	.45
15 to 18 inch	.60	.55
18 to 24 inch	.70	.65

BEAUTY BUSH (KOLKWITZIA) PINK

	Each
12 to 18 inch	.70
3 to 4 feet	1.25

BUDDLEIA (BUTTERFLY BUSH)

No. 1 Plants	.75

CALYCANTHUS (ALLSPICE)

2 to 3 feet	1.00

CORNUS (DOGWOOD)

SIBERICA (Bright Red Branched)

18 to 24 inch	.65

STOLONIFERA

2 to 3 feet	.70
3 to 4 feet	.85

CORYLUS AMERICANA (Hazel Nut)

	Each
2 to 3 feet	.80
3 to 4 feet	1.00
4 to 5 feet	1.50

COTONEASTER

ACUTIFOLIA

2 to 3 feet (B & B)	2.00
3 to 4 feet (B & B)	2.50

APICULATA

12 to 15 inch (B & B)	3.00
15 to 18 inch (B & B)	3.50

DIVARICATA

18 to 24 inch (B & B)	2.50
2 to 3 feet (B & B)	3.50
3 to 4 feet (B & B)	4.50
4 to 5 feet (B & B)	5.50

CYDONIA JAPONICA RUBRA (Red) (Japan Quince)

18 to 24 inch	.80
2 to 3 feet	.95

DEUTZIA

GRACILIS

18 to 24 inch	1.25

LEMOINE

18 to 24 inch	.85
2 to 3 feet	1.00

PRIDE OF ROCHESTER

3 to 4 feet	1.00

EUONYMUS

ALATUS COMPACTA (Upright)

15 to 18 inch	1.25

EUROPEAN

18 to 24 inch	.90

EUONYMUS PATENS, VEGETUS (See Broadleaf Evergreens)

FORSYTHIA

	Each	5 to 49 Each
FORTUNEI, PRIMULA, SPECTABILIS, SUSPENSA		
18 to 24 inch	.75	.70
2 to 3 feet	.85	.80
3 to 4 feet	1.00	.95
4 to 5 feet	1.25	1.20

HONEYSUCKLE (Lonicera) BUSH FORM

TARTARIAN (Pink): ZABELI (Red): FRAGRANTISSIMA (Winter Honeysuckle, White)

	Each	5 to 49 Each
18 to 24 inch	.75	.70
2 to 3 feet	.85	.80
3 to 4 feet	1.00	.95
4 to 5 feet	1.25	1.15

HYDRANGEA

	Each	5 to 49 Each
ARBORESCENS		
12 to 18 inch	.65	.60
18 to 24 inch	.85	.80
OAK LEAF		
12 to 18 inch	.85	
18 to 24 inch	1.00	
PANICULATA		
12 to 18 inch	.65	.60
2 to 3 feet	1.00	.95

LILAC

PURPLE, CHINESE, PERSIAN

	Each
2 to 3 feet	1.25
3 to 4 feet	1.50
NAMED FRENCH VARIETIES (Red, Purple, Pink, White)	
2 to 3 feet	2.00
3 to 4 feet	2.50

MAHONIA AQUIFOLIA (See Broadleaf Evergreens)

PHILADELPHUS (Syringa) Mock Orange

	Each
CORONARIUS	
2 to 3 feet	.85
3 to 4 feet	1.00
LEMOINE	
10 to 12 inch	.60
12 to 18 inch	.75

	Each	5-49 Each	50-100 Each
VIRGINAL			
18 to 24 inch	.75	.70	.65
2 to 3 feet	.85	.80	.75
3 to 4 feet	1.00	.95	.90

PRIVET

	Each	5-49 Each	50-100 Each
AMUR RIVER (North)			
12 to 18 inch		.20	.15
18 to 24 inch		.25	.20
2 to 3 feet		.30	.25
3 to 4 feet		.35	.30
GOLDEN			
12 to 18 inch	.50		
IBOLIUM			
12 to 18 inch		.20	.15
18 to 24 inch		.25	.20
3 to 4 feet		.35	.30
IBOTA			
12 to 18 inch	.40		
18 to 24 inch	.50		
2 to 3 feet	.60		
REGELS			
12 to 18 inch	.75	.70	
18 to 24 inch	.85	.80	
2 to 3 feet	1.00	.90	

PRUNUS TRILOBA

	Each
3 to 4 feet	2.50

RHODOTYPHUS (White Kerria)
KERRIOIDES
12 to 18 inch	.60
18 to 24 inch	.75
2 to 3 feet	.85

RHUS (SUMAC)
COPALLINA
3 to 4 feet	1.00

COTINUS (Smoke Tree)
2 to 3 feet	1.00
3 to 4 feet	1.25
4 to 5 feet	1.50
5 to 6 feet	2.00

GLABRA AND TYPHINA
5 to 6 feet	1.50
6 to 8 feet	2.00
8 to 10 feet	2.50

SNOWBERRY

	Each	5 to 49 each	50 to 100 each
CHENAULTI			
18 to 24 inch	.50	.45	
2 to 3 feet	.60		
RACEMOSUS (Whiteberry)			
12 to 18 inch	.40	.35	
18 to 24 inch	.50	.45	
2 to 3 feet	.60	.55	
VULGARIS (Indian Currant, Red)			
18 to 24 inch	.50	.45	.40
2 to 3 feet	.60	.55	.50

SPIREA

	Each
ANTHONY WATERER (Pink)	
18 to 24 inch	.85
ARGUTA (White)	
12 to 18 inch	.60
18 to 24 inch	.70
2 to 3 feet	.85
FROEBELI (Pink)	
12 to 18 inch	.60
18 to 24 inch	.75
OPULIFOLIA	
2 to 3 feet	.65
3 to 4 feet	.80
4 to 5 feet	.95
PRUNIFOLIA	
18 to 24 inch	.75
2 to 3 feet	.85
3 to 4 feet	1.00
THUNBERGI (Early White)	
18 to 24 inch	.75
2 to 3 feet	.85
VAN HOUTTEI (White)	
18 to 24 inch	.40
2 to 3 feet	.60
3 to 4 feet	.75

TAMARIX

HISPIDA (Pink) — Each

3 to 4 feet	.75
4 to 5 feet	1.00
5 to 6 feet	1.25

VIBURNUM (Snowball)

AMERICANUM (American Cranberry)

18 to 24 inch	.75
2 to 3 feet	.90

VIBURNUM BURKWOODI (See Broadleaf Evergreens)

DENTATUM (Arrow-wood)

18 to 24 inch	.75
2 to 3 feet	.90
3 to 4 feet	1.25
4 to 5 feet	1.50
5 to 6 feet	2.00

DILITATUM

18 to 24 inch	.85
2 to 3 feet	1.00

LANTANA

18 to 24 inch	.85

LENTAGO

18 to 24 inch	.85
2 to 3 feet	1.00
3 to 4 feet	1.50
4 to 5 feet	1.75
5 to 6 feet	2.50

MOLLE

4 to 5 feet	2.00
5 to 6 feet	2.75

PLICATUM

18 to 24 inch	.75
2 to 3 feet	1.00

SIEBOLDI

18 to 24 inch	.75
2 to 3 feet	1.00
3 to 4 feet	1.50

STERILIS (Common Snowball)

18 to 24 inch	.75
2 to 3 feet	1.00
3 to 4 feet	1.50

TOMENTOSUM

18 to 24 inch	.75

WEIGELA

BRISTOL RUBY (Patented)

18 to 24 inch	1.25
2 to 3 feet	1.50
3 to 4 feet	1.75
4 to 5 feet	2.00

EVA RATHKE

12 to 18 inch	.75
18 to 24 inch	.85
2 to 3 feet	1.00
3 to 4 feet	1.25

ROSEA (Pink)

12 to 18 inch	.60
18 to 24 inch	.75
2 to 3 feet	.85
3 to 4 feet	1.00
4 to 5 feet	1.25

WITCH HAZEL

18 to 24 inch	1.00

ROSES

(SPRING ONLY)

HYBRID TEA ROSES (Northern Grown)

	Each	Per 10	Per 25
Everblooming, blooms first year, strong two-year No. 1 plants, none better	$1.35	$12.50	$25.00

RED—Ami Quinard(darkest red); Christopher Stone; E. G. Hill; Etoile de Hollande; Grauss au Telplitz; Grenoble; McGredy's Scarlet; Margaret McGredy; Radiance Red.

PINK—Dame Edith Helen; Editor McFarland; Edith Nellie Perkins; Miss Rowena Thom; Picture; Radiance Pink.

WHITE—Caledonia; K. A. Victoria.

YELLOW—Golden Rapture; Joanna Hill; Mrs. E. P. Thom; Mrs. P. S. du Pont; Soeur Therese.

MULTI-COLOR—Autumn; Condessa Sastago, Duq de Penaranda; President Hoover; Talisman.

PATENTED HYBRID TEA ROSES

	Each	Per 10 Each
Charlotte Armstrong, brilliant red	2.00	1.75
Chrysler Imperial, deep red	3.00	
Crimson Glory, crimson	1.75	1.60
Eclipse, pure gold	1.75	1.60
Forty-Niner, multi-colored	2.25	2.15
Fred Howard, rich yellow	2.50	2.25
Helen Traubel. luminous apricot	2.75	2.50
Lowell Thomas, double canary yellow	2.00	1.75
Mirandy, dark red-black shadings	2.00	1.75
Nocturne, cardinal red-shaded crimson	2.00	1.75
Peace, golden yellow-shaded pink	2.50	2.25
Rubaiyat, large rose, red to crimson	1.75	1.50
Sutter's Gold, yellow-shaded orange and red, very fragrant	2.25	2.00
Tallyho, bright pink to crimson	2.00	1.75

POLYANTHA ROSES

(Baby Roses)	1.35	1.25

Else Poulsen (rose pink); Eutin (red); Golden Salmon; Lafayette (red).

PATENTED POLYANTHA ROSES

Betty Prior, red ,turning pink	1.50
Donald Prior, semi-double, bright scarlet	1.50
Fashion, coral overlaid gold	2.25
Ma Perkins, red and yellow, turning pink	2.25
Pinocchio, salmon pink	1.75
Vogue, cherry coral	2.25

CLIMBING ROSES

	1.25	1.15

American Beauty (red); Blaze (red); New Dawn (pink); Pauls Lemon Pillar; Pauls Scarlet (one of the best).

PATENTED ROSES, CLIMBING

Crimson Glory	2.00
Doubloon, copper and yellow (Patent 152)	2.00

PEONIES

(PLANT IN EARLY FALL — SEE FALL PRICE LIST)

VINES

	Each	Per 10
Ameplopsis (Boston Ivy)	.75	.65
Celastris Scandens (Bittersweet)	.75	
Clematis:		
Henryi (white)	1.00	
Jackmani (purple)	1.00	
Mme. Andre (red)	1.00	
English Ivy	1.00	.85
Halls Honeysuckle	.75	.65
Purple Wisteria Grafts	1.75	
Silver Lace Vine	.75	

FRUIT DEPARTMENT

APPLES

(Bold Type Indicates Summer and Fall Varieties)

Benoni, Cortland, **Delicious,** Dbl. Red Delicious, **Red Duchess,** Polly Eades, **Golden Sweet,** Golden Delicious, Grimes Golden, Hyslop Crab, Ida Red, Dbl. Red Jonathan, **Maiden Blush,** McIntosh, Northern Spy, **Summer Rambo,** Red Rome Beauty, Staymans Winesap, **Yellow Transparent,** York, Imperial.

	Each	Per 10
6 to 7 feet (extra size)	2.00	17.50
5 to 6 feet	1.75	15.00
4 to 5 feet	1.50	12.50
3 to 4 feet	1.25	10.00

DWARF APPLE—Delicious (red and yellow); Red Staymans;
Yellow Transparent; Red Wealthy 2.50

CHERRIES

	Each	Per 10
SOUR CHERRY		
First Class, Super Size (Montmorency)	2.50	22.50
First Class, Extra Size, Montmorency	2.25	20.00
First Class, 5 to 6 feet Montmorency	2.00	17.50
First Class, 4 to 5 feet (Montmorency)	1.75	15.00
SWEET CHERRY		
Black Tartarian, Schmidt's and Windsor		
First Class, 5 to 6 feet	2.00	
First Class, 4 to 5 feet	1.75	
First Class, 3 to 4 feet	1.50	

PEACHES

Champion, Early White, Elberta, Golden Jubilee,
Hale Haven, J. H. Hale, Red Haven
Shippers Late Red

	Each	Per 10
Super Size, 6 to 7 feet	2.00	17.50
Extra Size , 5 to 6 feet	1.75	15.00
First Size, 4 to 5 feet	1.50	12.50
Medium Size, 3 to 4 feet	1.25	10.00

PEARS

Anjou, Bartlett, Clapps, Duchess, F. Beauty, Kiefer, Seckel

	Each	Per 10
Extra Size, 6 to 7 feet	2.00	17.50
First Class, 5 to 6 feet	1.75	15.00
First Class, 4 to 5 feet	1.50	12.50
First Class, 3 to 4 feet	1.25	10.00

PLUMS

Bradshaw (blue); Burbank (red); German Prune (blue); Green Gage; Lombard (blue); Stanley Prune (blue.

	Each	Per 10
Extra Size, 6 to 7 feet	2.25	20.00
First Class, 5 to 6 feet	2.00	17.50
First Class, 4 to 5 feet	1.75	15.00
First Class, 3 to 4 feet	1.50	12.50

COFFING AND TALBERT APRICOT

	Each	Per 10
First Class, 5 to 6 feet	2.00	17.50
First Class, 4 to 5 feet	1.75	15.00
First Class, 3 to 4 feet	1.50	12.50
First Class, 2 to 3 feet	1.25	10.00

CURRANTS, TWO YEAR No. 1

	Each	Per 10
Fays	.60	.50
Red Lake	.75	.65

GOOSEBERRIES, TWO YEAR No. 1

	Each	Per 10
Downing	.75	.65

RASPBERRIES

	Each	5-24 Each	25-49 Each	50-100 Each
Cumberland (Black)	.25	.20	.15	.08
Indiana Summer (red, everbearing) Transplants	.30	.25	.20	.12
Latham (red) Transplants	.30	.25	.15	.10

BLACKBERRIES

	Each	5-24 Each	25-49 Each	50-100 Each
Eldorado	.25	.20	.15	.08

BOYSENBERRY (Spring Only)

BLUEBERRIES

3 year	1.50
4 year (bearing age)	2.00

ASPARAGUS TWO YEAR No. 1

	Each	5-24 Each	25-49 Each	50-100 Each
Washington	.20	.15	.10	.07

RHUBARB

TWO YEAR

	Each	Per 10
McDonald	.70	6.00
Victoria	.35	2.50

(Page Twenty-three)

PERSIMMONS

GRAFTED VARIETIES—Glidewell, Manly, Ruby

	Each
18 to 24 inch (B & B $ .60 extra)	2.00
2 to 3 feet (B & B $ .75 extra)	2.50
3 to 4 feet (B & B $1.00 extra)	3.00
4 to 5 feet (B & B $1.50 extra)	3.50
5 to 6 feet (B & B $2.00 extra)	5.00
6 to 7 feet (B & B $2.50 extra)	6.00

GRAPES

Agawam (Red), Brighton (Red), Caco (Red), Catawba (Red),
Concord (Black), Delaware (Red), Fredonia (Black),
Niagara (White), Worden (Black)

	Each	Per 10
Two Year No. 1	.45	3.50

STRAWBERRIES

(APRIL 1)

	Per 25	Per 50	Per 100	Per 500	Per 1000
Blakemore, little tart, large, splendid bearer	1.25	2.00	3.50	12.50	17.50
Dunlap, sweet, medium size	1.25	2.00	3.50	12.50	17.50
Dorsett, large, good bearer	1.25	2.00	3.50	12.50	17.50
Fairfax, good table berry	1.25	2.00	3.50	12.50	17.50
Premier, good size, good canner	1.25	2.00	3.50	12.50	17.50
Robinson, especially good for freezing	1.25	2.00	3.50	12.50	17.50
Streamliner, everbearing, best of all, excellent quality	2.50	3.00	5.50	22.50	

CPSIA information can be obtained
at www.ICGtesting.com
Printed in the USA
BVHW051459261118
534009BV00035B/3174/P